# The Portraits & The Poses

**Also by Edwin Brock**

*Invisibility Is the Art of Survival*

# The Portraits
# &
# The Poses

## Edwin Brock

A New Directions Book

Grateful acknowledgment is made to the above mentioned
publications and to the following publications and broadcast
organizations, where some of these poems were first seen or
heard: *Ambit,* BBC Radio 3, BBC-2 Television, *Mademoiselle,
New Statesman, Paris Review* and *P.E.N. New Poems 1971–72.*
'Collage' originally appeared in *The New Yorker.*

First published clothbound (ISBN: 0–8112–0486–3) and as
New Directions Paperbook 360 (ISBN: 0–8112–0487–1) in 1973
Published simultaneously in Canada
by McClelland & Stewart, Ltd.
Manufactured in the United States of America

New Directions Books are published for James Laughlin
by New Directions Publishing Corporation
333 Sixth Avenue, New York 10014

# Contents

## Rose Garden

The god-machine is on roses today
and I am trying to do my job properly:
'Red, Yellow, Pink' I say
'Blackspot, Rust and Mildew':
it is a tedious task making catalogues
and I do not know whether Orthocide
and Dithane are part of the plan.

I try very hard to appreciate:
'Red, Yellow, Pink' I say
with a catch in my voice and my face
arranged like Mary's at the Annunciation.
I am no fool: I have learned
when the bells ring and my hands are burned
from touching too many bare wires.

God has this good plan about roses
which requires only open eyes and a smile:
'Red, Yellow, Pink' I say, smiling,
for the burns are still there
and I would like to use my hands again.
Do you see how each rose offers you
its own colour, requiring only
that its roots shall feel some death
to feed upon, and that you should
die for it and enjoy the process.

God has this good plan about roses
and about people, that they should look
and smile and die and enjoy it. I am no fool:
'People' I say 'Red, Yellow, Pink'
and Mary and I have smiled until
every muscle in our faces aches and
we have tried enjoying it. But
our hands are heavily bandaged now

and sometimes at night I dream
that I have made it up. It is,
after all, something to do under the sun,
this looking at roses, it is something
to doubt; and with our hands bandaged
we can hold the wire and stare out
to where the world began.


## Accident

He just fell down
in the middle of the Saturday
shoppers who stopped
and stood and said
'He just fell down!
He just fell down!'
like a chorus in the High Street.

And it is a most extraordinary
thing that old people do
or have done to them
as though the earth needed
them like a magnet needs iron.

In his case
the pull came through granite
and he fell hard, breaking himself
when the soil reached for him.

In another time and another
place he may have fallen
softly, on old leaves
long grass or a ditch
full of weeds and stayed there
until the new growth speared him;
but he fell down in the middle of Saturday!

We do not like
this falling down:
our ambulances have bells
like lepers to warn us,
there are blankets to hide us and, far away
where we do not go
rows of white rooms
and strange white women.

It is an extraordinary thing we do
in the High Street in sunshine
forgetting what we were taught
seventy years ago:
to stand up, to sway
to make a line through time;
and when we fall down on Saturday
the shoppers stop, notice
and are amazed.


## My First Ghost

It was autumn
when my first ghost
danced down a hill

cold enough for anoraks
and a covering of leaves

but she wore silk
swirling as she hung
like Fonteyn
in the cold night air;

we were noisy
crashing through
branches and bracken

but she was silent
in a way that caused fear.

She was my first ghost
and I remember her
as I make ghosts
who do not dance
or swirl silk:

not waiting
for them to die,
I take them as they talk
or look
for life to happen.

Here in Norfolk
I stand at the sea's end
needing only a space
of six feet by two
to fill

and I make ghosts
like a drill sergeant
with poor recruits,
using lives
which have not
been lived in.

The trees hold their place
the pebbles strain against
their edges and the sky
and the sea are still:

my first ghost
could come here now
and dance among me
for I and all my company
do not endure.

## Fox at Winterton

All night the gale
had brought glass
wood and bodies
from the sea
using sand to make
a decent burial

leaving the beach
as ordered as
an Esher cemetery
each mound a mystery
except where a wing
or beak broke through
like weed.

I gave each one
a casual rite
dispensing death
like a clergyman
until I stopped
at a shape
as shocking as
a scream in church:

its red fur
stained the sand,
its head was chewed
into a fanged skull
and ten inches of rope
grew from its spine

yet enough of fox
remained to make
me flinch
expecting the massacre

to jump and snap and
infect my clean skin
with God knows what wounds

even walking away
I looked back
unless its stumps
stalked me along the beach:

not until another month
of tides had turned
its tame bones
would I accept it.

This creature contained
so much life
its death shrieked,
shaming the quiet cough
that takes us
so barely alive
the air settles
where we were
without a sound.

# The Poses

## Pose One

Often I dream
of shit in a tiled
urinal an institutional
urinal of walking
in it in bare feet
of sitting in it
of shit which will not
flush away because
every outlet is blocked
with the ooze of a
hundred bowels
and the torn remnants
of a hundred newspapers

these mornings my bath
stinks of Dettol
and every square inch
of my fat flesh
is indecent with
Wrights Coal Tar Soap

I breakfast with Ravel
Debussy César Franck
clean my teeth with
Beethoven and Bach
and take each sound to
prick tears

on bad days I pray
on the sharp shingle
of Cromer Beach
letting the North Sea
drain blood from
the cuts like
shipwreck notes

in old bottles
and tiptoe away
between the oil slick
and dead seabirds

I know at night
I will be there again
between the same
sweating walls
reading the notes about
John Brown's prick
and who's sucking it off
and in the morning
I will try the same
formula of art and prayer

it will never work
and one day I will
recognise it for what it is:
some kind of insight
on some kind of walk
to a place
something like Damascus.


**Pose Two**


I touch to make
a place to live among
and touching I unmake
what God began

I make all flesh words
to live among and
all flesh crawls nail-
damaged where I am

do you think I tear
for nothing? manageable
lumps of you disfigure
what I wear!

but if I threw you
finally to God
I could not bear
how he would leave you there.

It is night and I
am parcelling you together:
it is love, touch by touch
and hair by hair

until the darkness blows
where we are moving
and I dismember you
with a coward's stand:

I pull you from word
to flesh and flesh to word
until love and murder
are inseparable

and in the morning I use
your love like mortar
to make a headstone
for an epitaph.


## Pose Three

All the bridges are down
and I can only imagine
what the sides of the roads
resemble this morning

the season is irrelevant:
what if blossom camouflages them?
it is only flowers
feeding on old blood!

oh sure, that same birth-
death-decay story is still
going the rounds making
worms God's chosen people

but have you seen
how thin they are this year?
with so little living
there is so much less to rob.

I have a friend who stands
on the other bank shouting
'Be reasonable!' and he is, I think,
the population explosion

he has stepped into his
frame and does not notice
that he cannot
turn sideways on.

A light wind blows upon
this island carrying a
burning smell: at first
I thought it was fecundity

but I was wrong; now when I
switch power on in my house
the dust glows and the same
smell covers everything.

## Pose Four

This morning
the plain sea-surface
with nothing pre-determined

or into a simple wind
a bird throws those notes
with no intent

making a beginning

I am here
sickened by silences
and surfaces

saying I love
like the bird
its great arm reaching out

to where the god
leaves claw marks
raking along his side.


## Pose Five

After the wilderness
a girl in a mountain
was telling me
to lie down

I lost nothing:
the ground humped
as a whale swam under the hill,
people walked from the beach
to the waves,
and a man drew a crowd
by pulling nails from his hands.

Nothing happened;
the girl turned herself
into a storm
which asked me
if I was tempted;
the gulls dropped bread on us
and we were surrounded by sheep.

I remember it was October
and that when I stood up
she was still moving;
but there are plenty of travellers
on that road
and she was pretty.

Lower down
on the plain
everything was quieter

I couldn't think
what the temptation had been

and decided
I must have had
something else on my mind.


## Pose Six

No one has died
recently
but something leaves
gaps and their pain:

the wind moves
the noise stops
and I am shocked
to find nothing.

I understand seances,
needing the dead
to fill us out,
there is altogether
too much room
around everything.

Knowing death
comes in loneliness,
that hare
with a bare throat
has nowhere
in his life
to run,
or looks for
something familiar
and sees
behind it:

the wind moves
the noise stops
and he is shocked
to find nothing.

No one has died
but the stuff
the stars go through
grows inside us.


## The Great Pose

No more pictures,
unless the ghosts appear:
I am trying
to do without ghosts.

How many times
I've said one field
one tree and a broken hare
or stood on a beach
and taken one wave –

it's impossible . . .
I make the buggers up!
I've got a tree-
making hare-breaking
sea-machine in my head
turning out prototypes . . .
the *things* are never there!

And yet at this time of year
when the roads are empty
I come to this coast
like a hippy to a banyan tree
and stand on the cliff-edge
facing the sea
saying Do it, do it!

On the shingle below me
three men fish
a small ship takes forever
to cross the horizon
the wind blows gulls about
and two dogs chase
along the tide foam.
Do it, I say
and fix those men, that ship
and the dogs in memory.

For a time
I talk more life into them
than ever the wind or the sea made
until the weather changes and they fade
back into the machinery.

Oh I have fixed you and you there
staring as you talk
even closing my eyes
to see you better
and when I bring you back
you have more flesh
than I've felt before:

I have more dead cats living with me
than I ever owned
I have made more fathers
than made me
and all my gods have fine feathers
and strong arms.

I stand in the middle of this making
as frightened as a child
before pain
or rather it was the pain
took me there
and I am making the child
or perhaps the pain
is being nothing there
and contrarily I make it to hurt.

All these things are possible and happen.

It is tempting to call this a journey,
to stick both thumbs
in my grandfather's pocket and look back;
but always the sun yo-yos up and down
and nothing happens.

You, yourself, are nowhere.

Three men fish from a shingle beach
the wind blows gulls about them
and two small dogs chase a ship
across the horizon.

Someone has made something up.

And this, surprisingly
is the world's machine:
grass, flowers, birds and fish
are churned from our feet
without dread. Look, I am walking
in a small field; there is rain
on leaves and spiders webs; mice, birds
cows, lions and men steam in the sunshine.
Nothing approaches me. The field
is there forever and in a year
I may return to feel it.

Every weed has its own beauty
and not least because each year
it greens its straws;
white and yellow flowers appear
not to be seen but to seed; runners
reach out and rear up, couch grass
grows in my hair and my toes take root.

Now the field returns to me: mice
birds, lions and men steam in the sunshine.
I approach nothing and I am not approached.
But my fear falls and fertilises
and my loneliness loves.

# The Portraits

## L.E.B.

In 1965 you bounced
like a blonde Tigger
into a life whose
spring had snapped:

you began in a night-
club bouncing men
with bald heads;

you bounced a totem-
pole from the Old
Year to the New;

you bounced into
pregnancy into hospital
and bounced back

bouncing a baby whose
beginning could so easily
have been flat;

you bounced through
the Divorce Court bounced
a Judge off his bench

and bounced into home-
making as though the walls
were made of rubber;

you made sinning
seem merely a lack
of bounce

and when your time comes
you will leave us all
like a ball
we lost in childhood.

## S.J.F.B.

Eight years ago
we thought a white fish

so deep in its dark water
we did not see

until in its own time
it was ready

for us to know,
not knowing

it gave always
what was wanted

until it was given
and we knew;

we could not know
that someone

with those looks
and that way of being

would grow the way
you have grown

which we now know
by the way that

when you look or speak or move
a small white fish

splashes inside us
like a prayer.

# T.A.L.

There were always bombers overhead
when topless in old trousers
you played the Lost Chord
on a piano accordion
with your biceps

it was the same tune you played
when you punched the carthorse silly
and broke a navvy's nose
with the heel of your boot

what tunes you must have heard
and tried to squeeze through
that Swiss bauble!
Wagner at least
blew you through Burma
and back to break holes
in the bedroom door

and all the time you were playing
the Lost Chord and What'll I Do
When You Are Far Away

until, with the accordion pawned
you packed your bags and
rode to where we heard
the same tunes fading

and wondered whether it was
not knowing what to hum
made you break teeth
black eyes and leave weals
upon your daughter's bum
which now mark her womanhood.

# J.D.

ABA champion
nineteen twenty seven
with a cup in one arm
and your father
in the other

who fought Harry Mizler
knew Benny Caplin
and shared a bill
with Jack Peterson

for you my grandfather
mixed secret rubbing oils
for you the publican
made a gymnasium
and for you a pale nephew
stared in a mirror
and sneered at his biceps

twenty years after this picture
you punched your brother
into a drunken mess
and ten years later
helped us bury him

those few events
are all I remember
and all I require:

I make my myths
from such scant material
grubbing to find facts
to fit a present
which does not happen.

## J.E.B.

You are an uncomfortable
ghost, haunting eyes
chins and an elusiveness
around the nose;

skinny as a skeleton, your
dieting sons struggle back
to you for reasons you
would understand –

coveting the fashion gear
the flash shops sell
from The Elephant
to Walworth Road.

In fact, we are
so insubstantial
you could replace us
in flares and bright shirts:

nothing would have changed
and to change you from one
brood of sons to another
seems more than pointless.

You could easily join in
the jazz, the jokes and
sexual daisy chains
you left behind

and you would be more at home
there than trying to wear
the profundities
of anonymous bones
scattered on a London hill.

### G.B.L.

Your words have run down
as you sit mouthing
the lines in a TV show

as though a river had run
backwards from the sea
to peter out in a wet field.

Years ago I plugged my ears
with books and girls
to miss your Irishisms:

I played up Old Arry
as black as Noogitt's knocker
and held conflabs on streetcorners

while you watched
and mouthed and found
more words to murder

explaining that
everything I do
is just a phrase I'm going through.

## H.D. & F.D.

He swallowed raw eggs
floating in spiced vinegar

she crunched peanut brittle;

he had a stern portrait
of himself in the First War

she had fat holiday snaps;

he taught his sons to fight
upright like gentlemen

she bounced their children;

his bearing was like
an old Prussian gone to seed

her's like an Irish potato;

he cooked, gardened and shouted
at her whenever she tried

she grumbled inarticulately;

the family watched this performance
quietly taking sides

and afterwards laughed at the joke;

but once when she cried
I saw through the laughter

and when she died
he coughed for ten more years
without raising a smile.

## Happy Birthday everyone

Three men were hanging
on Penge Station, and I guessed
they would miss the eight-
fifteen. At Holborn Viaduct
a deep limepit had been dug
for slow schoolchildren.
I passed as I have passed
for thirty years: no bomb
came to London with my name on it
and when I stepped to school on
glass and plaster the bodies had gone.


Now it is Anniversary Time:
frozen Germans and gassed Jews
parade with banners, and Oxford Street
is festive with antique gibbets.
We use their flags to keep the weather
from our heads, proud that this
is History and we remember.


As usual the faces of new babies
pop as we tread over them:
there is much normality here.
My horoscope reads: Push ahead with
all your plans, everything is in your favour.


I push ahead with all my plans
on this frostbitten morning in July.
I know I am a man with a tamed imagination.
I have not yet caught a baby
on a bayonet. My employers trust me.
I will never die.

## From Chipping Norton

In these lanes
are edges
which are always damp

under an old stone
at the end of a wall
a mile between houses
where either grey creatures
start life or life fades
in cold grey creatures.

These hills in England
with green coverings
and stone journeys
grow numbness
at the ends of their extremities

as though that were the beginning
of a certain route
where we go
like a monk praying.

They are damp litanies
the voice croaks on
but sings:

the road rises and falls
turns and returns
but takes time.

It is a cold way
except where skin
closer than houses
forms wife, mother, daughter
and warms you there.

## Postwick Marshes

Spring shows
on this uneven green
the way the world
goes jump-mad

each step
kicks birds wing-
whistling from
the dips and

olympic hares
break from dyke
to wood in
even time

almost I feel it
and stop suspecting
God's plot
behind the sap

until the flying
and the singing
snap prayer back
like a snare

and I write the field
word by stinking word.
I will not go there
now to see

grass rotting
a hare fixed
and that idiot
who ploughs the peat

with a broken rod
panting to put life
into a landscape
he has paralysed.


## The Chosen

When they had gone,
the dog wagging
the children waving
and the wife running
to someone waiting,

he watched the sea
fuss along its edge
imagining its size
and its sickness:

the whales
eaten by dogs
the birds
by oil
and the bomb
rocking on its bed.

There was news
of a man leaving,
of children
torn by lions
and a woman sold;

that night the hills
fell into deserts,
there was a smell
of houses burning
and the jackals
returned.

When he thought,
it was that
there was nothing
to think about;
and about his feelings
there was nothing.

After the prophets
one god came
with a promise of love
but did not
offer happiness

so he took his possessions
to a white house
with a white doctor
and became a rich man
entering heaven.


## Prototypes

**I**

King George the Fifth
looked like my grandfather
and felt as close

when he died
I walked the streets
staring at houses

and their faces
to see if people
looked the same and

their homes still stood.
For a week
we were on the brink

of war or an earthquake
and when my mother
laughed at me

I abandoned her
to God's anger
or soldiers from the Tower.

King George the Fifth
was my first and last
king, his children

and their children
were never properly introduced
and I ignored them.


2
My father played the piano
with one finger of his right hand
and the fist of his left

he laughed at Gracie Fields
Max Miller and was away from home
for weeks at a time

when he died I cried
for my mother
and forgot.

I have never mastered the art
of becoming my father:
I have three children

pale jackets, suede shoes
and laugh at comedians
I do not admire

I stay away from home
for weeks at a time
but I do not resemble him

when he came home
he brought himself with him
and sat down

when I arrive
I hit the piano with both hands
and nothing happens.


**3**
Britannia glowed
from Empire Day
all the way to Barry Road

a big-girl jumped over
her skipping rope
and walked away on her hands

on Saturday night
I jumped over a saxophone
and ran among mad skirts

by Sunday I had married
the girl next door and all the saxophones
played the Last Post.


**4**
On my bedside table
is a triptych
of a king, a father and a wife

at night I sleep
with one eye open
hoping to surprise them

I am wrong:
their dead faces
fill all my gaps

and nothing happens
except I contain them,
father-king and dancing-wife

they have killed my ear
for saxophones
and nobody, not even

Fred Astaire, could take
his toes to a brass band
playing a requiem mass.


## Anniversary

Quite still . . .
I can take this hand
that eye
one hair in place
and place you there

in the morning there will be
smoke-mist on water
dampness on dead leaves
and the soil draining these away

in the morning
this hand that eye
and an early snail
quite still.

Already I have made
more than this:

you are in a room
with people
and occasions;
my daughter is suffocating
in a soft pillow;
our son's head as red
as his afterbirth:

these are the lies I make
to swear us by;

I would welcome a scream
or the sound you made
tapping along a drunkard's line
but that cut comes clean
above a nerve-end.

In the morning
there will be photographs
of mist on water
the first light pulling
our past away and
where I have placed you
an early snail
quite still.

## Curriculum Vitae

Often I said Our father
which art in heaven
using him to restrain
my father who
wert in home

the magic worked
until my father died
and the two were fused
confusing my mother
and myself.

This unhinged me
and after the scholarship exam
I abandoned him for
bicycles, filmstars, Glen Miller
and my penis

not knowing
that he was bringing me back.

Then smack in the middle
of my first unguilty orgasm
I cried My God! and he struck
with a shuddering from
the heart of the soft moon
I was in

which left me as lonely in love
as a desert father.

But that way needs two travellers
and my acolyte had gone in
a prayer where sex was sin
and I the wear and tear
of a woman's work

and my god whose beard had
worn a pubic point
died one frightened night
and did not rise again.

**44**

For years I looked for him
in Jesus Christ
and on Holy Fridays imagined
a plank of wood on Dawson's
Hill with a Nazi at the top

but I had seen too much and suffered
too little for that:

always I measured his pain
with the burning children and
their buried mothers who
had had no god to forsake them

whose death was permanent
in a London street and not
a long weekend in
a Mediterranean cave.

Either my god should have suffered
more or more simply made
no point of suffering.

And yet the moment
with the wafer worked

and the hooded monks
in their bare church

and the Nunc Dimittis
red with the sun
on a summer Sunday.

                *


a fat life builds
a flabby soul

its home neither
heaven nor hell

but a suburbia
where both are foreign;

at this stage of infancy
one starts again:

there are no angels
in the trees

but sometimes
the light falls to show

something behind some
thing behind something.

The land is lonely now
it is a lonely land

one grass grows
where there were two

and in the desert
even sand shrinks;

when I pray
it is that I will find

in this field
I have come to

something behind some
thing behind something

like the dream
of a tree still growing

or the sound
of a rat among reeds.

## Quiet in Norfolk

**1**
Here is a clear case
for surgery:

for keen knives
in clean hands
in tampered air.

All life this field
has made a claim
on therapy

where trees ducks
and one frenetic hare
played doctor:

it is no place
to bring a child
posing question
upon question

where one weak god
can talk of nothing
but love.

Better cut the cancer bare
to a clean bone where
the air will be white
and silent –

in a month the scar
will be unremarkable
and white on white
the silence will bear me out:

one hare will crawl
without cover
one duck will stare

and reluctantly
these reeds will renounce
an unnecessary song.


**2**
There is an obedience
of silence:

a mouse flies quietly
in an owl's beak

a fox dies dumb
in a dog's teeth

and on a skull's hill
God withdraws
when his sons call.

Row on row
in white beds
an isolation of flowers
and the season's fruit
make a tidy loneliness

where we move
in crowds
behind music
or quietly
about a landscape
which is suddenly ours.

We do not believe
there are others screaming
nor that if each mouth
sounded
the wind would break its stillness
and the waves compete again.


**3**
A late hour
of guillotined flowers
and a truncated message!

Caught in the corner
of a cut field
trees sky and creatures
are hounded

and in the ploughed land
only small burrowing things survive.

Always at this time
love comes down like seamist:

something to crawl behind
imitating the pain call
of a hawk on a pole trap.


## Summer Visit

All our maps have these small crosses
with an arrow at the top
to show where God went:
something about birds falling
trees bending, rain, hail and snow.
Down here I keep it behind glass
to switch on and off like a toy.

Forty years darkness is thick here:
rain has fallen and in damp places
fingers grow. My mother blinks
in sunlight, her roots making cracks
I can never explore.

I am afraid. This place is not
situated but grows around
wherever I am. Sometimes
I make it move and move into it
pretending to be real.
My mother watches and waits to begin.

Nothing changes: voices and weather
drift in the same direction.
A mad dog climbs the kitchen wall
and dies. A coffin is balanced
between two chairs. The sky
is low and flat and my mother's noise
fills the space beneath it.

Time shrinks and stretches without
rhyme or reason. I am the child
I saw in a seaside snap: I make
donkeys move, hear my mother
call and let memory happen.
Nothing happens, except the tapeworm
fear between us eats and grows fat.


## Collage

I have made
a grey fish
still on a slope
of fine sand

his white lips
frame and close
a black hole
on and off like
a neon sign

when his fins flutter
a puff of sand
supports him
and settles again:

this is an event.

I have made
a white bird
a gull
whose yacht hull
slides across
a surface
I cannot see

his mind is gathered
between wingtip
and wingtip following
his lost eyes:

I leave him there.

I do not collect
time:
bird and fish
will be still
until I return:

God is on my side.

I travel
to meet a man
with light hair
and a photograph

I plan
a loved woman
by his side
and skip between

I hear breathing
along cool lanes

one child held
in the high note
of a known song:

this is history.

I am afraid
of the way
these pictures
dry:

I am tired
of creation.

I have no time
for the fish
to flash from
rock and sand

for the bird
to be unleashed
from wingtip
and wingtip

the child must
remain between
that woman and
that man sung
in a high note.

Living
I make this
perpetually
to be alive

it is
an uncomfortable way
to make a living.


## Words for Bird Sea and Rock

Between
bird flying
water moving
and rock

is something
I put my mouth to
and suck
God

       *

Bang on the slap
of each fifth wave
a bird circles

on each fifth
circuit the sun
breaks rock

at night
this picture stays
still until
sunrise

only I move it
believing it
exists

truth is a matter
of making stones
move like curtains

as I make this
preferring a
predictable death
to another strange
resurrection

*

Bird
strung on the end
of my hand
you make dying
possible and

for this suffer
only the bending
of one straight
line

it is necessary
that you are
clipped and tethered

54

that you come
in with the tide
and take me out

without that
I would learn
wave-walking
ass-riding
persecution and
the face of God

it is easier
to turn you
about me
and call your
sad mewing
music

\*

Bird opened
its beak
to the sea
shrieked
and leadened
by this syllable
fell

all death
is timely
prayed the words

imposed upon
the shore
like a dead star
watching.

## Five Exposures

**I**
I remember
low sunlight
flaring
on high windows
as though
photographers
were out of sight

and a war:
black photographs
on flat paper:
desert
and jungle
town and snow

that is all
I remember
the rest
is certificates
and children.

Sometimes at night
my skin remembers
more than
photographs
but I am not
deceived

I have seen
photographs
of felt skin
and there was
no memory
in it.

**2**
The town stood
over snow
deserts and jungle
rumbled
out of sight

footprints led
to high windows
flaring in
low sunlight

in children's voices
there is only
hindsight
growing its own
pictures

what I remember
is silent.


**3**
I am in love
with this photograph

we are
round sun
sharp stars
certificates
and children

history has us
here in a
flat surround

making us move
is a poet's
preoccupation
as pointless
as fossils
on a long beach.

The wind blows
until I feel it

the sun shines
until I look

there were children
before I knew them:

the point is
that days go
through my eyes
and die there

I am a great
disclaimer

superstitiously
I touch prayer
to make
a photograph
for God
to love.

**4**
For twenty years
I tried for
one touched object

and gathered objects
in square rooms
under a battery
of lights

but made only
this photograph
of high windows
in low sunlight

where we are
round sun
sharp stars
and children:
windless
voiceless and
out of sight.


**5**
Poetry is not
love
nor is there
poetry
where love
has been

felt skin
freezes on
flat paper
and there is
no memory
in it.

Children run
through snow
and the houses
take them in

the town stands
over snow
and is black
on flat paper

this is today
and tomorrow is
where this
has been

under my eyes
the days die
and are printed

the round sun
sharp stars
and children
have not lived.

## Four Landscapes with a Gull

**I**
Looping
like a halo
glittering
his light head
she drew him
out to sea.

I was three:

so close to the tide
it deafened
so unending
that I cried

until my mother
rescued me
and I forgot.


**2**
She does not
forget I forget:

even between two
parents
breaking bread
in the Sunday park

she swooped again
scattering choirboys
in her surplice dive
grabbing one warm
piece of flesh
shrieked
and was off

leaving me alive.

**3**
I do not know
if I forget:

sometimes it seemed
closing my eyes
she blotched
the clean horizon
with a white spot

or leaving England
was hovering astern
with other birds
held between them
like a cold cross

I do not forget.


**4**
I had forgotten:

this morning
back-broken in
a hopeless bed
white as the snow
outside
I watch her
threaten my window
in suicidal dives

wanting it open
wanting my guts
for her garters
and my eyes
for her prize.

## History

Over and
over some
thing like
wind is
whipping
through our
two conifers

as though
the walls
had allowed
crows in
or perhaps
the sky
had decided
against us.

And I really
did know
a man who
ran amok
with knives
and was
certified

(he was
a quiet man
who played
with my
daughter
and mended
bicycles).

Now that
he has gone
the wind
is no less
and over
and over
the crows
accuse us
with knives

nothing is
ever defined.
Mostly
I make
my life
leave on time
and carry me
home again

the crows
fly quietly
in my pocket

the sky
is undecided

and my daughter
no longer
plays with
men who
mend bicycles.